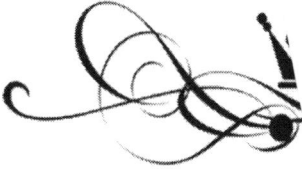

Stop Worrying

How to Start Living in The Present Moment, Eliminate Negative Thinking and Become a Happy Person Again

Andrew D. Hoskins

Your Gift!

We want to show our appreciation that you support our work, so we have put together a gift for you.

Just visit the link on the last page of this book to download it now.

We know you will love this gift.

Thanks!

Table of Content

Introduction

"The oldest and most powerful human emotion is fear, and the oldest and most powerful fear is the fear of the unknown."

(Howard Phillips Lovecraft)

When we are children we think, the world is a beautiful, fair place, where everything is right and we can become what we want without any effort.

When we are children we are rewarded for every action and we believe the world is perfect.

But when we become adults we understand that the world is difficult, it is a dirty and cold place, and we start to be scared. The fear of being humiliated, the fear of not being able to relate to others, the fear of not being able to realize a project, the fear of success or failure, anxiety and panic.

Fear has many forms but has only one result, fear prevent us from living our lives in the best of ways. Some people are literally paralyzed by fear and they can not overcome that trauma in any way, while other men do not know how to handle certain situations.

Managing fear is extremely important in our society, especially in relation to other people. The world is a difficult place and we must use all our courage to survive and achieve results. Except for some privileged people who born rich, no one gives anything for nothing and we have to fight with our nails and teeth to get what we want.

Imagine being prisoners, the condemned of a comic strip with the black and white uniform, and you have a big ball at your foot, which prevents you from escaping. First you have to freeyourself from the ball, otherwise you will not be able to escape.

Fear works like that big ball of steel tied to your ankle, which prevents you from moving one step. Getting rid of the ball is vital for those who want to live a successful life or just accomplish what they want.

The point of the speech is that you don't need to be ambition to overcome fear. Fear can prevent a person from going home, going to a supermarket, or reading a book. By preventing these daily activities, it is impossible to live our lives normally, and thus eliminating fear must be a priority.

Overcoming fear is very important both for the CEO of a multinational and for the young college student.

In more severe cases fear can turn into anxiety and depression, as well as in panic attacks. In that case, a doctor's intervention is absolutely necessary.

In this book we will observe how to get rid of the chains of fear and come back to live our lives. You will find that it is very easy with the determination and willpower, and one day you will laugh at everything that scare you now.

The fear is afraid of being defeated, we are going to scare her!

Chapter 1: What Is Fear?

"The biggest mistake in life is to always be afraid of making mistakes."

(Elbert Hubbard)

People are fascinated by fear.

The horror genre is always working to create new movies can scare anyone and Stephen King's books are worldwide best seller.

Somehow people love to be scared when they look for entertainment, maybe because they know it's all a fiction. They know that Leatherface will not come out of the screen to kill them (though his story is inspired by a true story, just like "Psycho" and "The Silence of the Lambs").

But when we talk about real life, no one wants to be frightened. Maybe someone wants to feel strong emotions, such as doing skydiving, but nobody does not want to be afraid.

But what is the fear?

With this term identifies different states of emotional intensity ranging from a physiological polarity as fear, apprehension, worry, restlessness or hesitation until a pathological polarity such as anxiety, fear, phobia or panic.

The term fear is then used to express either current emotion or anticipated emotion in the future, or a mere state of concern and uncertainty.

Usually fear is represented by a sense of unpleasantness and an intense desire to avoid a dangerous object or situation. Other constants of the experience of fear are the tension that can reach to immobility (being paralyzed by fear) and the selectivity of attention to a small portion of the experience; In fact, we can hardly remember the scary experience completely. This focus on consciousness leads us to obsessively observe that situation that frightens us. The experience is negative, pervaded by insecurity and desire to escape.

Where does the fear come from?

From the results of many empirical researches we come to the conclusion that potentially any object, person, or event can be perceived as dangerous and thus induce an emotion of fear.

Variability is absolute, even the threat may arise from the absence of an expected event and may vary from moment to moment to the same individual. Essentially, fear may be innate or learned. The key factors, however, remain the perception and evaluation of the stimulus as dangerous or not. There are two types of fear, innate and learned.

Innate fears originate from a number of factors, which are:

- Intense physical stimuli such as sudden pain or noise.

- Items, events or persons unknown. We do not know how to behave with them and this creates uncertainty.

- Situations of danger to survival. They are often inherited from our ancestors or from modern situations, such as fear of height, cold or abandonment by a family member.

Examples of typically innate fears are: fear of strangers, fear of the dark, fear for certain animals (spiders and snakes), terror at the sight of amputated human anatomical parts.

The fear learned is the result of a series of stimuli or experiences that have proved to be ugly or dangerous.

The universal mechanism responsible for acquiring learned fears is termed conditioning, which can turn any neutral stimulus into phobic stimulus, by pure association with an originally source of fear stimulus.

For example, if we had a bad experience with a dog, we will most likely be scared of all dogs, because every animal will remember that trauma.

Fear manifests itself in many ways, for example with the famous "terrorized" expression, or eyes closed, half open mouth, close eyebrows, frowned forehead. This state of tension in the facial muscles represents the expression of fear that is well-known even in the early age and in the different cultures.

Body reactions to intense fear states, such as panic and phobia, and those with deals with worry and anxiety are different.

Precisely, a state of acute and sudden fear of panic and phobia is accompanied by the activation of the parasympathetic autonomic nervous system, there is a decrease in blood pressure and body temperature, decreased heart rate and muscle tension, abundant sweating and dilation of the pupil. The result of this activation is a kind of paralysis, namely the inability to react actively with the escape or attack.

The function of this staticity seems to defend the individual from aggressive behavior triggered by escape and movement. Paradoxically, in extreme cases, this parasympathetic reaction can lead to death by cardiovascular collapse. States of less intense fear instead activate the sympathetic nervous system, so the hair grows, the muscles flow more blood, and the muscle tension and the heartbeat increase; the body is so ready for action or escape.

What is the function of fear?

It surely serves to signal a possible danger of preparing the mind and body to what may happen, and fear can immediately alert any other person near us about the danger.

In summary, it is a defense mechanism that man improves with the evolution of the species, often the fear of something prevents us from doing stupid and potentially damaging things. Fear is triggered by our brain to prevent us from hurting.

By learning how to handle fear correctly we can handle it and exploit it to avoid potential dangers, but when this feeling is overcome and we are unable to handle it and becomes anxiety and panic, resulting in an unmanageable danger where intervention is needed a specialist.

Chapter 2: Begin to overcome fear

> *"One day the fear knocked on the door. The courage went to open and found no one."*
>
> (Martin Luther King Jr)

Overcoming fear is a long and complicated process that takes time and different approaches.

In fact, there are people who do not literally fear nothing while others are afraid of their own shadow.

Why?

First, we have to consider the physical appearance of a person. A tall, muscular and strong man will certainly be less afraid of

other people because he can use his physical appearance to win fights, impose his will or just to discourage a malicious person.

No one would attack Arnold Schwarzenegger or Mike Tyson. Instead, a small, minute woman with a slim body is naturally more likely to be afraid because she has no physical means to discourage the aggressor or to defend herself in the best way.

We also need to consider the education and the social environment where a person grew up. Growing in a wealthy and safe neighborhood will allow these people to not be afraid of the outside world because their environmental model is safe and secure.

In addition, personal experiences are the factor that can make a difference.

Any episode can create a deep fear within us, which we can not defeat in any way.

My personal story with two examples.

When I was a kid, I was hiking with my kindergarten on a beach, and suddenly a fierce summer thunderstorm came in, with lightning and thunder. My teachers put us immediately into the bus and went home.

The coach was absolutely sure, and the storm ended instantly, but the trauma of seeing the sky full of lightning continued to scare me for years.

Every time I saw a flash or listened to a thunder I started to cry very hard and tremble with fright.

My mother and my grandfather began to talk and console me, and at the end my grandfather invented a story to explain the origin of thunder and lightning.

"The thunder is the noises created by the quarrel between the devil and his wife The devil is struck by beads in his head"
That simple explanation made me laugh, and fear disappeared.

My grandfather unknowingly used one of the best systems to defeat fear, that is to ridicule her.

Making something ridiculous is a way of reducing its importance and enhancing its flaws, as happens in satire.

Making the object of your fear ridiculous will help you understand that fear is totally unfounded and counterproductive, because it will only prevent you from living your life the best way.

So stop being scared of the monster, and start to tease it. You'll find out it's just an imaginary monster.

Often our fears are only in our head, in a psychological or physical way, and for that I would like to tell the story of SM. Who is SM?

SM is a woman who is not afraid of anything. She is not a superhero or an imaginary character, but she is an American woman who can not feel the fear.

She can walk among the snakes with absolute tranquility, stroke the back of hairy spiders and numerous other

adventures that would scary any other human being. No, she is not an extraterrestrial or even a robot ... she is a woman of almost 50 years old that is suffering from a rare illness that has completely destroyed the amygdala. That is the small structure of the brain that deals with emotions, especially fear. The task of the amygdala is to control, like a sentinel, every situation in search of a real or imaginary threat. To do this, compare the current situation with those in your emotional archive and ask the question: "is something I fear, hate, that can hurt me?" If that question gets an affirmative answer, it sounds the alarm bell by sending an alert to all parts of the body.

In the case of SM, all the fears have vanished ... this might seem a wonderful thing if it was not that all the fears related to real threats that SM learned during her childhood have disappeared, for example not talking to strangers, beware when she cross the street or do not insert her fingers into the electrical socket.

The message I want to convey with the SM's story is that fear must not be perceived as a totally negative feeling. Fear acts at an unconscious level to protect us from any dangers and has helped man in all its evolution. Fear has evolved over time, our ancestors were afraid of the animals and the dark, we are afraid of ISIS and the theft of our computer data.

So fear is a negative feeling, but it helps our sixth sense to avoid doing stupid things.

The problem arises when we can not manage fear properly and this feeling becomes too strong, preventing us from doing anything. For example eating one muffin each day is not a bad thing, but it becomes a problem if we start eating 4 muffins a day.

Be prudent and to behave cautiously, avoiding to go into dangerous situations, like walking in empty and dark places at night, is a clever behavior, not starting a project for fear of failure, instead it is a strongly negative behavior that needs to be corrected immediately .

The failure of managefear properly results in ruin our lives and prepares the path for anxiety and panic. The problem needs to be resolved immediately, but you do not have to think of becoming "Daredevil, the man without fear" but just know how to handle your fears properly.

If you are a person with a natural tendency to frighten you will never become Rambo, but still you will learn how to handle the problem effectively.

Even in this case there are no shortcuts, but only willpower and will to improve. There is no miraculous medication or sanctification in personal growth, but only commitment and knowledge of your mind.

So if you're sick of being afraid to realize your project, or if you can not speak in public because you are afraid of the reaction of the crowd, began this journey with me, and see who overcome fear is really easy and quick.

First, is necessary a theatrical gesture with a great motivational impact, which I have already illustrated in the book about procrastination, the Bruce Lee method.

Bruce Lee looked like a fearless man.

He was courageous, strong, capable of facing every enemy and every challenge in the best way. But that was just his public mask and the character of his films.

Bruce Lee, in his private life, was a common person with fears, dreams and aspirations. Bruce created a highly effective motivational gesture to defeat his fears, such as accidentally injuring himself on the set or hit his colleagues too hard.

Bruce wrote his fears on a sheet of paper, so he analyzed them.

You shoud take a sheet of paper and a pen, and analyze sincerely yourself (sincerity is the basis of all my methods) and write down all your fears.

After writing them all, take the sheet and burn it in front of you.

In this way you will symbolically burn all of your fears, erasing them from the mind.

The second part of the method consists in analyzing the fear, and transforming it into a growth opportunity.

For example, you wrote: "My fear is to be fired."

Well, even I have this fear, and I think 90% of the world population have the same fear.

Then analyze this fear by asking you these questions:

Do you like your current job?

Is your wage appropriate to your time and commitment?

Is this work the job of your dreams?

Would you want to do that job for 35 years?

Do you think you deserve better?

Answer honestly and in this way you will defeat the fear.

Maybe you hate your job but you're also scared to look for a better one. Wage is low, but you think a little money is better than zero.

This fear of being fired could happen, but turn it into an opportunity for growth. You will find a better job and you will succeed. Each door that closes opens a larger door. Fears should not block you and prevent you from realizing your dream.

This system suits every type of fear.

"I'm afraid to stay single." Well, are you satisfied with your relationship? it is better to be single than to suffer for a complicated relationship.

"I'm afraid to stay without money." Analyze your expenses and find out that you can manage your budget and buy everything you want and saving money at the same time.

Every fear hides the opportunity to improve ourselves and defeat them.

Fear is often cowardly, and she knows that we can beat her easily and for this reason she exacerbates all our fears. Fear wants to live inside us, but if we can turn these thoughts into opportunities we have won the war.

To finish the chapter it is clear that defeating fear opens the door to many new growth opportunities, because:

- You'll have more freedom.

- You will be much happier.

- You will have the opportunity to take advantage of new opportunities for growth.

Chapter 3: How to turn off the fear.

"If there is a solution because you worry about it? If there is no solution because you worry about it?"

(Aristotle)

Every person is different and every person has his or her own individual fears, so defeating fears does not follow a fixed method because each person has a personal fear management approach that has been influenced by his or her education, the environment where he or she grew up and the life experiences. In cases of unmanageable fear such as anxiety and panic, it is necessary to ask the help of a professional and the use of medicines, this is why this chapter is only for informational purposes.

Despite the individuality of fears there are universal systems to start dealing with fears in the best way, to take note of the problem and to initiate the resolution path of the submitter.

   1) Become aware of your fears

Use your loyal sheet of paper and check your list of your fears once again.

The first step is awareness, that is, take notice of fears and accept their existence. At this time you do not have to think about defeating them but just to analyze them.

Every fear has a source, first you have to think about the motivation that caused it and the way to solve it.

Another personal example: During my work one day a load of furniture overwhelmed me and I almost broke the dock, the result was to be locked in bed for a month. In that case I was lucky because I could end up on a wheelchair if the furniture had hit me in the back.

From that moment on, the fear of wheelchairs was born inside me because they reminded me of that risk. First I took notice of my fear and then I faced it thinking that I was lucky and that I can still walk. I have scared the fear in a sense of gratitude for my good luck.

Knowing and accepting a problem is the first step to defeat it. We are not perfect and no one has the right to criticize us for our fears, because there is no man who is not afraid of something except SM.

2) Distinguished between useful fear and harmful fear.

As mentioned earlier, the amygdala, the person in charge of fear, can also act if it is not in the presence of a real threat. It is interesting to note that the acronym for Fear in English can also mean "False Evidence Appearing Real".

In this regard, think about how much time and energy you have reserved in the past to fears that were never fulfilled. Fortunately, in fact, it seems that only 5% of these tents come true, so it is very likely that what you fears is not a real threat. Useful fears are the ones that make you stay away from real dangers and keep you safe, such as the fear of burning you if you get too close to the fire. Bad fears are what you have in response to something imaginary that is not a real threat to your safety. Examples of imaginary fears are: the fear of speaking in public, the fear of mistake, the fear of the judgment of others.

Crossing the street without looking could be a serious threat to your safety, a negative comment to a person about what you did or said no. Unless you are attending bad friends or extremists on Facebook.

Start by then to see if your fears present real threats to your survival or are just imaginary scenarios created by your mind without any real dangers.

But fearful fears can become real fears, especially those related to the computer world.

A comment on Facebook can be seen by many people can attract hate and negative reactions, and can turn into a real danger, or the theft of data we leave on social networks or the Internet.

This does not mean that all harmful fears can become real, but we must not even isolate them from the world and pretend that they can not become real dangers.

3) Prevent, solve, and turn off the alarm bell.

If the situation involves a real threat, just take the necessary action to prevent it or solve it, and if fear is not real, just turn off the fear switch.

There is a method that is specialized in turning off the alarm bell of a bad fear, called CORE Technique, and is the best method to overcome this kind of fear.

Chapter 4: CORE Technique

"Fear can not sleep. It's always awake."

(Anonymous)

What we call fear in reality, like any other emotion, is nothing more than the moving energy in our body.

A sometimes-used definition that I really enjoy for the word emotion is indeed Energy-in-Motion.

Words like fear, anger, joy, etc are just the language labels that we use to describe the characteristics of the emotional energy we experience in our body at a given moment.

When our brain faces a danger, emotional energy is generated in our body that has strong mental and behavioral repercussions.

At our brain does not care if the danger is real or imaginary, he frees the feelings of fear whenever it senses danger, both true or imagery.

This is a problem, especially when these feelings are about an

imaginary danger, that is, a danger that is not intended to damage us physically, for example the fear of speaking in public, the fear of others, or the failure of an exam.

Nobody will get hurt with this fears, because they are only a mental threat.

From childhood we tend to avoid unpleasant emotions, adopting different suppression and evasion strategies. Unfortunately, these habits, although they can bring momentary relief, do not eliminate fears and make them stronger.

Avoiding dealing with a problem is never a smart solution, because hiding the problem will make it bigger and sooner or later you will have to deal with it, like it or not.

The body is smart and makes us feel the same emotion in front of the same stimulus, until this fear is not "resolved." What do I mean by resolved? By resolution I mean "disconnecting" irrational fear from the stimulus that triggers it.

It is possible to intervene in more than one way and on different levels over fear and other emotions.

We can do this, for example, through energy psychology techniques, with cognitive methods such as Pnl and hypnosis, and through somatic interventions linked to the use of conscious attention and the resulting emotional integration. I think that in most cases the elegance, simplicity and minimalism of this last system cannot be beaten.

Throughout our lives, we often think about past experiences, and over time, this habit favors the accumulation of an entire archive of incomplete emotional experiences in us. Our body reminds us, however, taking care of these emotional debris by continuing to produce the same kind of energy in front of the same stimulus until it is fully processed.

That is why if you have a bad experience with a wheelchair, your mind will remember you every time you see one, until you solve the problem.

To eliminate fear we must therefore allow ourselves to fully experience the emotional energy associated with it until its completion.

And this is why I'm introducing the CORE to you.

The author of the technique is Tom Stone, an expert in developing new techniques for solving emotional trauma and fears. He is the founder and CEO of the Great Life Technologies that provides support to war veterans and their families.

The technique devised by Tom is called "Core" "Center of Remaining Energy" and consists in bringing our awareness to the center of emotional energy trapped in the body to fully experience it. The opposite of what we are conditioned to do. Incomplete emotional experiences are made of energy and the center of this energy is very similar to a cyclone.

The intensity is greater in the center and decreases going to the outer sides.

With the technique you will allow yourself to come into contact with the most intense part of the energy. It 'an experience that may look to jump with a parachute in the eye of the storm.

The more you approach the emotional epicenter, the emotion will become more intense, but when you get to the center you will feel suddenly calm and you will find that the safest place is right in the center of this emotion.

Applying this technique takes a few minutes a day, but this does not mean that CORE is simple.

Here are the five steps to correctly apply the CORE technique.

Step 1: Recognize your fear.

Close your eyes and think about the situation that evokes fear in you. Attention: It is important to start with a situation that does not evoke a very intense emotional reaction.

Step 2: Give a vote to the intensity.

Vote sincerely by calculating the value of intensity of emotion. 0 represents no fear, while 10 is the greatest fear ever.

Step 3: Locate the emotion in your body.

Scan your body and notice what part of it experiences the emotional energy associated with this fear. You might notice it, for example, in your belly, chest, neck, etc.

Within the area in which you experience the emotional energy, find the point where this is more intense, the epicenter of the emotion.

Step 4: Use the laser.

Your awareness is like a laser beam. Point this laser beam into the epicenter of emotion and concentrate all your attention there until the intensity disappears.

Step 5: Dissolve all

In a metaphorical sense it is as if your consciousness "absorbs" the emotional energy trapped in your body. This may take a few minutes, allowing yourself time to fully experience all emotional energy, avoiding distraction or following some thoughts.

At some point, it may happen that the area where you experience energy moves from the starting point, in this case, you just have to continue to identify the most intense point and "zoom" on it with your awareness as long as energy emotional is completely dissolved.

This technique takes time and effort to be fully functional, but here are some little tips to learn how to handle it.

Do not force the time.

Every technique takes time to be executed to perfection, so do not rush, and take your time. A relaxed and positive attitude is undoubtedly very useful.

Start with simple emotions.

One of the light emotions to start, so learn how to handle the CORE.

Do not lose focus and not stop the treatment at the first signal of relief.

Conclusion

"Do at least once a day something that scares you."

(Eleanor Roosevelt)

Here's the infallible way to get rid of fear.

This system is suitable for any kind of emotion, fear is a useful feeling, but only if it can handle it. We must not allow any emotion to ruin our lives and we must always be in full control of the situation.

Fear is afraid of us, because we can defeat her, if we want.

Your Gift!

We want to show our appreciation that you support our work, so we have put together a gift for you.

bit.ly/2xXbHO5

Just visit the link above to download it now.

We know you will love this gift.
Thanks!

Printed in Great Britain
by Amazon